All About Me

MY HOME

Walls,
Floors,
Ceilings,
and Doors

Written by Lisa Bullard • Illustrated by Brandon Reibeling

Content Advisor: Lorraine O. Moore, Ph.D., Educational Psychologist
Reading Advisor: Lauren A. Liang, M.A.
Literacy Education, University of Minnesota, Minneapolis, Minnesota

PICTURE WINDOW BOOKS
Minneapolis, Minnesota

For my Caitlin-L.B.

Designer: John Moldstad
Page production: Picture Window Books
The illustrations in this book were prepared digitally.

Picture Window Books
5115 Excelsior Boulevard
Suite 232
Minneapolis, MN 55416
1-877-845-8392
www.picturewindowbooks.com

Printed in the United States of America.
1 2 3 4 5 6 08 07 06 05 04 03

Library of Congress Cataloging-in-Publication Data
Bullard, Lisa.
   My home : walls, floors, ceilings, and doors / written by Lisa Bullard; illustrated by Brandon Reibeling.
      p. cm.
   Summary: Caitlin and her father, an architect, plan and build a house for Lulu the dog. Includes suggestions for drawing a floor plan and making a model house.
   ISBN 1-4048-0046-8 (lib. bdg.)
   [1. House construction-Fiction. 2. Fathers and daughters-Fiction. 3. Doghouses-Fiction.] I. Reibeling, Brandon, ill. II. Title.
   PZ7.B91245 Myg 2003
   [E]-dc21
                                                                2002008606

Hi! I'm Caitlin. Daddy and I are going to build a house. It will have walls, a floor, a ceiling, and a door—just like my house!

3

Daddy is an architect. He dreams up new buildings. He draws pictures called floor plans to show the builders how the rooms fit together.

I want to be an architect, too. Daddy says it's a good idea to start small, so we're going to make a doghouse for Lulu. Her house will have just one room.

Lulu's house doesn't need to be very big. That's because she spends most of her time in my house. We eat dinner together in the kitchen, and we watch TV together in the living room. Sometimes she sleeps with me in my bedroom.

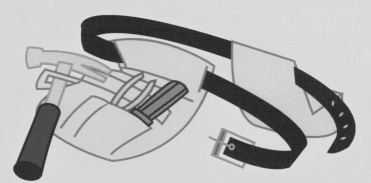

Before Daddy and I start building,
we clear a place in the backyard
big enough for a doghouse.

Daddy saws some wood
into doghouse-sized pieces.
Then we start to build.

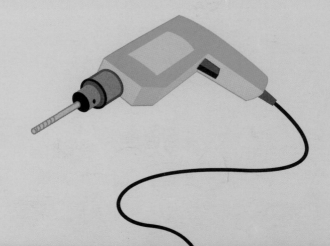

First, we put down the floor where Lulu will sleep. The floors in my house are good for tap dancing and for holding up the furniture. I want Lulu's floors to be that strong.

Next, we add walls to keep the wind from blowing in on Lulu. Sometimes when I play, I'm really loud. Then Daddy says he's grateful our house has such thick walls.

Finally, we nail a roof on top to keep the rain out. I wish the roof kept the thunder out, too.

Lulu and I will decorate her house together. I might put glow-in-the-dark stars on the ceiling. We could paint the walls purple, like the walls in my room.

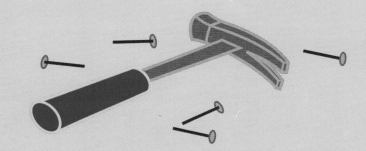

Lulu's house is shaped like a box. It has a pointed roof on top and a hole for the door.

My house is shaped like a bigger box and has a bright red front door. It has two floors connected by stairs. The funny thing about stairs is that they go both up and down.

Did you know that houses come in different shapes and sizes?

Some people live on boats that float on the water or in mobile homes that can be moved. Other people live in tents, sort of like the one we use when we go camping.

My cousin Claire lives in an apartment.
She and her family have their own
rooms and their own front door,
but they share a roof with all
their neighbors.

Claire's apartment is way up on the
fifth floor. I like looking out Claire's
windows. We can see the park two
blocks away.

Apartments and houseboats and mobile homes all sound like fun. I asked Daddy which kind is best.

"Any home is best, if you live there with someone who loves you," he said. I guess that makes my house the very best home for me!

Activity #1: Drawing a Floor Plan

What would your house look like if you could make it just the way you wanted it? To draw a floor plan, you'll need a pencil, an eraser, and some paper. Graph paper works best; it has little squares already drawn on it. Each little square is the same size. If you don't have graph paper, use any other kind of paper.

1. Think about the rooms you want in your house. Which room will be the biggest? Which rooms will be next to each other? Will there be hallways or closets between any of the rooms? Where will the doors be?

2. Study the places you and your friends live to get other ideas.

3. Begin drawing your floor plan on your paper. If your house has more than one floor, draw each floor on a separate sheet of paper. You may have to erase a lot—or make several drawings—until your floor plan looks right. Even real architects make mistakes sometimes.

4. Once you have figured out the floor plan of the house, you can draw in furniture and add color to the rooms.

Activity #2: Making a Model House

A model is something made to look exactly like something else, except smaller, like a model airplane or a model car. To make a model house, you'll need one or more shoeboxes, scissors, glue or tape, markers, and colored paper.

1. Take the cover off your shoebox. The cover of the shoebox will be your roof, if you decide to have one.

2. Draw doors and windows on your shoebox. Ask a grown-up to help you cut out the doors and windows with the scissors.

3. If you want other rooms for your house, glue or tape several shoeboxes together. Make sure to cut doors between your rooms.

4. Use markers, paper, and other craft materials to decorate your rooms.

5. If you want to see the rooms inside of your model house, leave the cover off the shoebox. Otherwise, you can place the cover back on your house for the roof. If you have used more than one shoebox, cut and tape the shoebox covers to fit on the boxes so you have one big roof.

Words to Know

apartment–a home that has its own rooms and front door, but which shares outside walls and a roof with other apartments

architect–a person who plans what new buildings will look like and decides how the rooms will fit together

ceiling–the upper, inside surface of a room

floor plan–a drawing showing how all the different parts of a building will fit together

houseboat–a boat that people live in, with places to cook, sleep, and relax

mobile home–a home on wheels that can be moved from one place to another

To Learn More

At the Library

Gibbons, Gail. How a House Is Built. New York: Holiday House, 1990.

Morris, Ann. Houses and Homes. New York: Lothrop, Lee & Shepard Books, 1992.

Rylant, Cynthia. Let's Go Home: The Wonderful Things About a House. New York: Simon & Schuster Books for Young Readers, 2000.

Thermes, Jennifer. When I Was Built. New York: Henry Holt & Co., 2001.

On the Web

FamilyFun: For information on fun family building projects
   http://family.go.com/homegarden

Sesame Workshop: Play games and explore the world.
   http://www.sesameworkshop.com

Want to learn more about homes?
   Visit FACT HOUND at http://www.facthound.com.